WITHDRAWN

watch it come down

watch it
come down

OHN OSBORNE

FABER AND FABER
Queen Square
London

First published in 1975
by Faber and Faber Limited
3 Queen Square London WC1
Printed in Great Britain by
Latimer Trend & Company Ltd Plymouth
All rights reserved

ISBN 0 571 10854 7 (hard bound edition)
ISBN 0 571 10855 5 (paper covers)

CAST

SALLY PROSSER

BEN PROSSER

RAYMOND

GLEN

SHIRLEY

JO

MARION

DOCTOR ASHTON

act one

The action takes place in two separated areas of what was once a country railway station. At the back of the larger section is the door leading to the deserted platform and station, which can just be seen through one of the windows. Also deep countryside in distance. On one side, what was once the booking office has become a dining-room hatch. The main part of the set is obviously what was once the entrance to the station and waiting room. The smaller section, separated by a door, may have once been the parcels office. This is where GLEN *is at present. Beside him, as he lies in a very large comfortable bed, covered in blankets and pillows, is a pile of books from which he is making notes. In fact, there are books everywhere, and in both main rooms, although more in* GLEN'S. *Near him, in a comfortable old armchair is* JO, *reading and eating an apple. They both look content. She is strong-looking, about thirtyish, sharp, open and a spirit of natural inquiry about her. He is considerably older, with a comfortably frail look of some of those who lead a bookish life but there is an amiable fever there too.*

In the main room, SALLY *lies on a large rug talking to* RAYMOND, *who is propped nearby. She is somewhat older than* JO, *carelessly smart and definitive looking in contrast to* JO's *glaring sloppiness which some might take to admiringly and others leave thankfully alone.* RAYMOND *is in his late thirties, the quiet, dog-of-all-work homosexual who pads reliably at the heels of others' lives.*

The old station has been done-up with some care but it doesn't quite come off. It's been made to be as comfortable as possible, almost like a penthouse in parts, but odd concessions have been made to its origins in the odd gas lamp here and there and the odd timetable or bench. There's even a touch of railway green in places. However,

9

BEN *has his say about this later. On one side, there is a set of steps, leading to* BEN's *mother's room. On the other one to* SALLY *and* BEN's *room. There are also doors to where* SALLY's *sister,* SHIRLEY, *works and sleeps. Also one for* RAYMOND.

SALLY: Ben must have been barmy to buy this place.
RAYMOND: Well, it was cheap, right in the country, and lots of room for people.
SALLY: People! He hates '*people*'. Who 'lives' here? Me and him—if you call that living. His old mother so's he can shove her up above the booking office with her television and cats. His father because he didn't have to have *him* much either until he was dying and he started treating him like Tolstoy on *his* last platform. An academic old pouf who lies in bed most of the day writing waspish biographies to scandalize and titivate his friends who write for the weekly newspapers—when he's not being wise and famous and discreet with his boys in the old parcels office.
RAYMOND: He could still use the old 'Gents' on the platform if he wanted.
SALLY: I expect he does. But he's the only one who's as nice and encouraging to Ben there is. Encouragement at his age and after what he's done! Most brilliant young director at Cannes, revolutionary. Even his Oscars didn't corrupt him! You're here, my sister's here because I can at least talk to *you*, when he can't or won't or doesn't. Jo's here because she looks after Glen and his 'writing' and because she's the sort of randy tongue-in-the-lip romantic Ben thinks he missed out in his search for the Holy Groin. As long as he lusts after her he feels the odd flicker of life even if they do threaten the almighty constant standby power cut. You're here because he's doing me a favour having someone to talk to and he can feel generous and big too because he knows you don't go for girls. Also, he doesn't really like you. He only likes old-style, exotic or bitchy, brainy poufs. Shirley he allows to do her old painting here—which he more or less openly

10

despises even to her—because he still has a daft, mystical itch that she might be the enigmatic tally to me. He doesn't really believe it, but it helps to flesh out a pretty dull scenario. If he did get to bed with her, he'd find acres of hand-picked, morning fresh peas under that mattress! He doesn't want that kind of trouble even if he does toy about with it. It wouldn't be soft or cuddly for long. He's doing me a favour, letting me have girl-talk with my own sister through the two-way mirror, both so alike, both so different. The hard form of enigma! And me? Why am I here?

RAYMOND: You love him?

SALLY: Yes. Sort of. In a way. There's always been a tiny fuel in the tank. Or a dribble in the can to crawl home.

RAYMOND: Doesn't sound much fun.

SALLY: It isn't. Do you know what *is* fun any more? I used to think I did. It's rusted up. By people like Ben. All seriousness and newspapers. No frivolity. Not honest, easy, unthinking frivolity. How to be frivolous and impress everyone . . . I don't think I ever really liked him.

RAYMOND: You must have done.

SALLY: Why? People marry for love. You don't have to like 'em. That's Ben's mistake. I like you. Yes, and I love you. That's what's Ben's sure-fire one, this is it, wait for it: If your fag friends are so great and appreciative and affectionate and you can 'talk' to them, why don't you——

RAYMOND: Marry them——

SALLY: Marry them! *Our* sex pitch has been washed out for years. Why don't you become a *real* married nun?

RAYMOND: I'm sorry.

SALLY: Oh, he exaggerates. So do I. 'Rhetorical' he calls it. But *he does*. Some fishy self-importance about being Celtic or Coptic or something . . . Ending up in a self-conscious tarted-up Unlikely Homes Supplement railway station. What am I doing in a bloody railway station! A caravan would be better. Intimate community living.

Nothing to do. Except bottle fruit and make vile wine, like Jo, and try and explain ourselves to odd journalists from comfortable houses in Islington or Wembley why we're as barmy as they think we are. 'The Prossers, tired of the rat race'—I wasn't tired, I was still in my stride— 'decided to change their life style, get away from it all as so many of us would like but lack their initiative.' Initiative! We could have had a Palladian gem for the graft we bled out to bolshy, careless, barricade-minded builders for this railway folk-weavers' folly. No one to see . . . I almost wish Will Hay would walk in with Graham Moffat under his arm. Except that Ben would go into some mad, menopausal ecstasy and then I'd *have* to leave. I wish the trains *did* still come through. I could throw ham rolls at the passengers.

RAYMOND: There's still one a week.

SALLY: Only a goods train and that's closing down next month. Ben says then he can get on landscaping the gardens. Gnomesville. Halt! Water gardens from the ladies' loo and potted plants in the signal box.

(*A small train goes through.*)

RAYMOND: Well, *there's* your weekly ghost train.

SALLY: Get *out*, someone! Even if you're a ghost! Ben'll be home soon.

RAYMOND: Would you like me to tell the others first?

SALLY: What? About us separating? Ben and me?

RAYMOND: Yes.

SALLY: Sure.

RAYMOND: You've made up your mind?

SALLY: Yes. Tell my sister. Tell Jo; she'll love it, tell Glen. Needn't bother with Ben's ma. It won't worry her, just so long as her cats are fed and the telly's working.

RAYMOND: I just wondered.

SALLY: What?

RAYMOND: Well, as it isn't *true*. About you both separating.

SALLY: Who knows? It might be. It almost is. Perhaps it will be. Perhaps they'll all jolly it along. Should be interesting. Their concern, I mean.

RAYMOND: Has Ben agreed?

SALLY: Not really. Of course, he's intrigued with the situation but he had heavy moral scruples, oh, all about putting one's friends to the test and conspiring against them and playing some hideous truth game . . .

RAYMOND: Then perhaps I shouldn't.

SALLY: You do what *I* say. And act as if *you* think it's true.

RAYMOND: *Should* I!

SALLY: Why not? He doesn't like you? You'd better tell my sister first. I can get her out of the way more easily. Then Jo and Glen. And make sure they're all going to be very English and discreet. Not that they won't be all looking like a bunch of misused basset hounds. Can't wait for his ex-wife to find out. Marion'll be down like a *shot* if she can. I wonder if she went to lunch with him and the child today. Not that he'll tell me the truth. Where is he? Probably mooning over the old boy's grave after a touching lunch with his small daughter.

(*Enter* BEN *from the platform. He is in his mid-forties with the look of a man who has tried fitfully to look younger but only partially succeeded.*)

Lunch all right then?

BEN: All right then. Whatever that means. Hello, Raymond.

SALLY: What about me?

BEN: What about you?

SALLY: Yes. Well, a kiss or just 'Hello darling, couldn't wait to get back . . .'

BEN: Oh, I could wait all right. I spend my life waiting.

SALLY: So you say . . .

BEN: Like Queen Victoria you always lead from well in front.

SALLY: Oh, blooming quotations. One of Glen's, I suppose.

BEN: Yes, another. Better than your unlistening, constant rant.

SALLY: My——

BEN: To continue——

SALLY: Oh, we *have* had a bad day . . .

BEN: Like Melbourne, you have great capacity for love. And nowhere to put it.

SALLY: Thanks a hump. (*To* RAYMOND.) Impressed? He's read

13

a book.

BEN: And forgotten them all.

SALLY: Well, they certainly didn't teach you anything. A spot of gardening would have done you more good . . .

BEN: You only accept love. You can't respond to it . . .

SALLY: Do shut that bloody door. That platform's like a wind tunnel. You always come back pompous when you've been to London. Why didn't you buy a new set of gear, a suit or a new shirt?

BEN: I didn't have time.

SALLY: Well, you are getting too portly for clothes, I'll agree. You're boring poor little Raymond and he's been such fun.

BEN: Gay, you mean.

SALLY: Oh, shut up, bitch-face.

BEN: We know what that's like. Being GAY. Whoops! The shroud of spontaneity!

SALLY: Don't overdo it. At your age, you can't. Anyway, it makes *you* look like a *real* pouf.

BEN: I'm sure. It could fool *you*! Sorry, Raymond.

SALLY: You're not sorry. You like saying hurtful things. They require no effort. You're just boring *him*. And what's worse, me. The minute you get in.

BEN: Sorry. Carry on carousing.

SALLY: You've put the clappers on that all right.

BEN: I've had a long day.

SALLY: All the days are long the way we live. It must be something to do with the shifting ice-cap. Or maybe it's just you?

BEN: Oh, knock it off for five minutes. Do your cabaret somewhere else.

SALLY: You wouldn't believe it but it goes down quite well with some people.

BEN: Oh, I believe. There's always a public for vulgarity and cruelty if it's put over well. Try the working men's clubs. Or the Black Rhinoceros; a literary lunch; or an evening at *Giselle*.

SALLY: Giselle—'e's 'ell.

14

BEN: *I* thought that was funny when *you* were learning to make omelettes and speak French in Switzerland on Daddy's hard inherited shareholdings.

SALLY: Don't leer at my father. At least he was brave and never whined.

BEN: Perhaps he should have. Anyway, I liked him. Oh, here we go . . .

SALLY: Yes, here we go. Mr. Wonderful Wise Man. Anyway, he didn't like you.

BEN: So you say. Often. It doesn't really matter.

SALLY: No, he's dead. He saw through you.

BEN: Well, he was successful on the stockmarket and the racecourse.

SALLY: Why shouldn't he be? He was bright and interested in things.

BEN: He was. Is there a drink?

SALLY: At least *he* could hold his liquor. The *hard* stuff. Not like you.

BEN: I remember. The Colonial Service was the spearhead of his chota pegs.

SALLY: Oh, not that! At least we didn't all slobber ourselves to death with requiems and odious music hall songs at *his* funeral. I suppose you had a misty-eyed butchers at his grave on the way back?

BEN: I looked in. Dammit, it's only a month.

RAYMOND: Here's a drink.

BEN: Thanks.

SALLY: 'And yet within a month.' Well, say 'thank you' properly.

BEN: I don't know what 'properly' is.

SALLY: Evidently. But don't brag about it. My father was *interested*.

BEN: He was.

SALLY: I don't know why. He wouldn't be now.

BEN: Just as well he's not here then. Cheers to the departed!

SALLY: Getting all those people down to that sickening funeral. He *died*; that's all. Not before time. I think even *he'd* have been embarrassed at your turning it into a Ben

Prosser production.

BEN: He liked a bit of carnival, anyway.

SALLY: Boozing and sponging you mean. He didn't even like *you*.

BEN: No?

SALLY: No.

BEN: What do *you* know about it?

SALLY: A lot. He used to talk to me quite often. In an incoherent, illiterate sort of way.

BEN: Did he? Is this for Raymond's entertainment or mine?

RAYMOND: I'll pop upstairs.

SALLY: No, you stay. Just because His Regisseur Droopy Drawers has dropped in.

RAYMOND: I've got to see Shirley.

BEN: No, no, stay. You can see what she has to put up with . . .

SALLY: We've *all* had a long day. Get *me* a drink, Raymond, darling.

BEN: Darling!

SALLY: What's wrong with that—darling? (*Pause.*) Let me take your coat off.

(*He looks at her suspiciously but lets her do so.*)

Mustn't let you get yourself cold . . .

(RAYMOND *gives* SALLY *a drink.*)

RAYMOND: How was the journey then?

BEN: Oh, fine. Had a row with that Major Bluenose.

RAYMOND: What about?

BEN: Oh, usual. If he and his wife see any of our dogs on their land, etc., he's offered £5 to any of his men who shoots one.

RAYMOND: Lovable man.

BEN: Oh and our cats worry his sheep. Sheep! And his heifers! And some stuff about layabouts lolling about here.

RAYMOND: Layabouts! What about those yobbos smashing up the windows here last month? Bet he arranged that.

BEN: Living in the country! All ex-housemasters, rear admirals, prying vicars, prowling group captains, ladies with walking sticks and scarves, tombolas, pony events and the *Daily Telegraph*. And they wonder why we won't go to their sherry parties! Sherry!

SALLY: I don't know why you're surprised. I grew up in it. The people are just more common and self-conscious, that's all. After all, it *was* your idea to get away from the messianic miseries of metropolitan Albion. The town is *people* and having to *give way*. The country's not green much and rarely pleasant. Land is bad for people. The green belt of muddied, grasping, well-off peasants from public schools and merchant banks.

BEN: Look who's talking!

SALLY: *I* know what I'm talking about. With shotguns in the woods, tea and pearls, rural swank and a tub of money under the chintz four-poster. Fetes opened by local TV celebrities, restoration funds, old ducks who 'come in and do', village greens, hunting 'manners', indifferent food and pewter candlesticks, over-healthy children home for the hols, greedy Gorgon nannies, undergraduates fumbling behind bushes of floodlit lawns, dancing till dawn with Miss Sarah Crumpet-Nicely of Grasping Hall while Mummy and Daddy look on at all the young people 'having such a good time' against this nasty, brutish issue of English Country Life. No, there's not much life in the land. Fish and animals yes; and the pigs who *own* it and *run* it.

RAYMOND: Well, can't say I've seen much of that.

SALLY: Don't worry. You won't. Except as somebody's bit of a lark. Not a lower-middle-class pouf from Leicester and living with a lot of nuts in a railway station. No, land is for the truly covetous. They'll even let armies of Japs and Texans loose on it to slaughter the pheasant, the grouse and the deer and have a Wildlife Vietnam of their own to keep what they've got. Mindless millionaires wading in the jungle warfare of the new-style trout stream——

BEN: I think you've made your point. I'm almost beginning to see theirs.

SALLY: You would. You're a snob.

17

BEN: Yes. Could I have another, Raymond?

SALLY: Why can't you get it yourself? What is he—the butler?

BEN: Only for some, I dare say. (*He goes to refill his glass.*)
(*Pause.*)

SALLY: And how was lunch with your little daughter?

BEN: She's not little—as you know. She's eleven years old and
over five feet tall.

SALLY: Really. I forgot. I'm surprised *you* remembered. Well?

BEN: Well, what?

SALLY: Lunch. *The* lunch with little—sorry, tall—*fruit* of your
tired old loins?

BEN: Look! I'm just back. Do we have to keep this up straight
away?

SALLY: Sorry. Did you say *get* it up or *keep* it up?

BEN: Getting coarse a bit early, aren't we?

SALLY: As usual, I take my cue from you.

BEN: Cue. The only cue I'd give you is a billiard cue. To
break over your head. I'm tired.

SALLY: So am I. You *must* think of others.

BEN: I have.

SALLY: And I thought your memory had almost failed alto-
gether. What did she eat? Five feet one. Face like a bun.

BEN: I don't know. It can't interest you.

SALLY: Of course it does. I wouldn't want to have a round
little—sorry, *tall* round—step-daughter.

BEN: Steak, spaghetti, ice-cream and coke. All right.

SALLY: Bad for the figure and the teeth I'd say.

BEN: It's what she wanted. It wasn't for me to argue.

SALLY: You're her *daddy*, aren't you? But it's hard for you to
come down even a bit heavy. After all, you did leave her
—a little—a little *tall*—baby for a lady who wasn't her
mummy. *And* who's only a step-mummy.

BEN: You're hurting yourself . . .

SALLY: No, I'm not. I'm past all that long ago.

BEN: Well, perhaps I'm not.

SALLY: Ah . . . Did you see her *Mummy*? Mummy: very
attractive, in a stunted sort of way.

BEN: Stop it, Sally!

SALLY: Stop what?

RAYMOND: Another drink?

SALLY: Yes. Give the Master another drink. He's had a hard day. Mummy's a very witty woman at the dinner table. She says things like 'Hemingway's mind was never raped by an idea.' Awfully good. She says it quite often too . . . Did you fuck her?

BEN: No . . .

SALLY: Pity. It might have cheered you up. Before coming back to Country Life Halt and old Dad's grave. I'm sorry you didn't enjoy your lunch *à deux*. Not much to say to one another?

BEN: Damn it, I only see her about three times a year . . .

SALLY: Difficult to communicate? That's sad. There are so many things little girls are interested in. Especially when their daddies are famous, like film directors. I always find she never stops chattering when she's with me.

BEN: I've no doubt.

SALLY: Perhaps you've never cared for the secret of getting through to other people—even little girls. Even your own tall little girl . . . Or perhaps she doesn't *like* you. Just that . . . A lot of people don't, you know . . .

BEN: Will you, you, will you, for one minute, just stop that fucking pile of shit spewing out of your fucking mouth!

SALLY: A hit, Raymond. I say: a *palpable*!

BEN: Or you'll get my fist right in the fucking middle of it. From my puny fist even if it breaks my arm . . .

SALLY: You mustn't damage your arm . . . Can *I* have another drink?

BEN: I'm sorry.

SALLY: No, I'm *sorry*. I shouldn't have said those things. It's my fault.

BEN: I—I, well, bad time . . . But I bought you a present . . .

SALLY: Thank you. That was sweet of you. I'll open it after I've, I've had this . . .

(*She takes a drink from* RAYMOND. BEN *gets his package.* SALLY *sips the drink and slowly slides into a low moan of tears.* BEN *looks on.* RAYMOND *puts his arm round her—nods to* BEN, *who slowly puts down the package, and walks upstairs to their room. He hesitates half-way, as if to go back over to her. As he starts back,* SHIRLEY *appears from her doorway, closely followed by* JO. *When* BEN *sees them he returns back up to the room.* RAYMOND *looks round quickly and motions both girls back.* SHIRLEY *also falters but then goes back.* JO, *however, stands watching the scene for a few moments without moving. Then slowly, she goes back into her room, closing the door behind her.* GLEN *looks up.*)

GLEN: Anything the matter?

JO: Nothing . . . I'll get us some tea in a minute. (*She strokes his hand.*) Glen, darling . . .

GLEN: What's that?

JO: You really are so very gentle . . .

(*He pats her hand affectionately. Meanwhile,* RAYMOND *comforts the collapsed* SALLY.)

CURTAIN

SCENE TWO

Shortly after.

RAYMOND *comes down the stairs from* SHIRLEY'S *room.* JO, *unseen, is in the kitchen preparing* GLEN'S *tea.* SHIRLEY *is upstairs in her room. So is* BEN'S MUM: *vague telly sounds. Her voice calls out* 'Ben, Ben! Are you back? Where *is everyone . . . Is there a cup of tea? Cup of* tea? . . .' *Then silence.* RAYMOND *looks around, then looks to* GLEN'S *door. He knocks.*

RAYMOND: Am I interrupting?

GLEN (*rising and picking out a couple of books from the surrounding piles*): No, come in.

RAYMOND: Thought you'd be kipping.

GLEN: Not a bit. As a matter of fact, I think I'm on the last page of my book.

RAYMOND: Then I'd better leave it.

GLEN: No, don't, my dear. After twelve hundred pages and three years I should know where I'm at. The most enjoyable bit. Topping it off with the right coda, *and* knowing what it is . . . Something's wrong, isn't it?

RAYMOND: Yes.

GLEN: Sally and Ben?

(*He returns to his sofa and box with books and manuscript.*)

RAYMOND: Yes.

GLEN: We heard them scrapping of course. But it didn't sound special. Well, of course it's always *special*. We're all that . . . What is it?

RAYMOND: They're: splitting up.

GLEN: Again?

RAYMOND: Yes, but *really*.

GLEN: What will they do?

RAYMOND: She's leaving . . . You know how she hates this place.

GLEN: I've heard her say so. But I thought she liked this bizarre warren enough to stick it out. I always thought the country was good for novelists . . . Not women perhaps.

RAYMOND: She says she hates the land.

GLEN: Ah, I know what she means. It doesn't always bring out the best in us. Suspicion, cupidity, complacency, hostility, profiteering, small, greedy passions, tweedy romance, all that. Beef barons, pig and veal concentration camps, Bentleys and pony traps and wellies. The Country. It's the last of England for *them*, the one last, surviving colony. This is England, all the merchants and adventurers and district officers have all come back. They don't want a new flag going up, a new name for their nation, all coal fields and oil riggers, Coventry, plastic factories and Dagenham Man. The fuzzy wuzzies from Durham and the Rhondda are at the last gate . . . How *did* it happen? They needed one another. But no more. Who's going? . . . Is this really *it* this time?

RAYMOND: Sally? Seems certain.

GLEN: Certainly it's no place for an intellectual like Sally. Or Ben. Where do any of us go now? When I started this book I thought we all still needed what was even left.

RAYMOND: You and Jo love it here.

GLEN: I had my salon life in London which could accommodate everything, the metropolis *and* the country as well as blimps and lefties—the snobberies of both. Enough good food, drink, sex, drama, gossip, frivolity, gravity, friendship, bitching and charity which dared to speak its name. *Ah, Albion qui n'ose pas parler son nom.*

RAYMOND: You know I don't speak French.

GLEN: Just as well. A harsh way of saying commonplace things. Of making platitudes sound like paradoxes. I've been guilty of doing it all my life. It was only a precious bon-bon which I'd never dare even utter to Ben . . . So, it *does* all fall apart. Hardly surprising when there's hardly ever been a centre and certainly not ours. We've seen the future *and it doesn't work* . . . I might give *that* to Ben. He'd like the sentiment anyway. I think I shall take a rest somewhere. Where can one afford to? Even a bachelor, like me, with no responsibilities. Die? That's pretty expensive if you're not snappy about it. I haven't the energy for suicide. I don't mind the melodrama because mercifully one doesn't have to witness it.

RAYMOND: Don't joke, please, Glen.

GLEN: Armageddon's a better laugh than Dunkirk. Do they *really*——

RAYMOND: Yes. What about Jo?

GLEN: She doesn't need to care for me. Oh, she needs to love me. But she needs real love. While there's time left for it. Not just sex. She's open to anything. It's her magic and her misfortune. But magic more, far, far more. Sally can write a novel about her life with Ben in between cocktail parties and love affairs. Ben can brood over whether to ever direct another film for the next mere anarchy. And whether to send that vile old mother off to a senior citizens' home at last and kill off her vile pussy cats, have an affair with Jo or Shirley or Jo and Shirley, go back to his ex-wife—which I hope he doesn't—or just blunder into some other form of chaos. *You* can go back to the rag trade, I suppose. Or will you stay with Sally?

RAYMOND: What do you mean?

GLEN: Stay with Sally?

RAYMOND: I don't know what you mean. I came here to look after Sally and Ben, do the cooking, shopping, household chores, the animals. What are you getting at?

GLEN: I can't see you doing the same thing with Ben on his own. With *both*, yes. So, will you stay with Sally?

RAYMOND: She hasn't asked me.

GLEN: I'm sure she will. There'll be other Bens. If she does go.

RAYMOND: Well, I just, well, I was asked to tell you.

GLEN: By Sally?

RAYMOND: Yes.

GLEN: Does Ben know?

RAYMOND: I think so. I haven't spoken to him.

GLEN: I see. Am I to refer to it? Or carry on as usual?

RAYMOND: I don't know.

GLEN: Ah: play it by ear. A bad option for me. I can't abide conspiracies.

RAYMOND: Well, I'll let you finish.

GLEN: It's only another book. Books are an outmoded form of communication. Probably fascist from what I hear from my old University. Perhaps they could turn it into an old folks' home for people like Ben's Mum. Think how they'd enjoy sitting in their wheelchairs in the College Gardens and watching telly in the Senior Common Room.

RAYMOND: Trouble is you're a snob. Even if you do like taking home guardsmen.

GLEN: Of course I'm a snob. Just like some people are pigeon fanciers. And young guardsmen, believe me, Raymond, have always been the fancy of many an upper class queen. It does take a certain amount of coinage— like marriage. At least, guardsmen are smart, alert, with bodies like fleshed out greyhounds. That's how I got my beautiful family nose broken and the stitches over my eye. That's why I never fancied you, Raymond. Just tight trousers, a bad, working-class skin, all huff and pouf.

RAYMOND: *Some* people like it.

GLEN: Some people will put it in a brick wall, I believe.

RAYMOND: Finish your bloody old book. I've done my job.

GLEN: Who else have you told?

RAYMOND: Shirley.

GLEN: Ah, yes. *Painting* at her painting. Isn't it time she had another rally? Or stuck humanity's sharp banner up some police horses' inciting arseholes?

RAYMOND: Yes, you *are* a pig. I like her paintings; they're violent. They're about *now*!

GLEN: It must be a paler point in history than I thought. And my coda *is* wrong.

RAYMOND: You're an old, old before your time pouf pig, stewing about in past glories and handing down all that in lofty 100-page indexes.

GLEN: You've been peeking. Found your tongue today. Not Sally's.

RAYMOND: *I* know what I think.

GLEN: What about Jo?

RAYMOND: She's my next.

GLEN: Just a moment——

RAYMOND: What?

GLEN: No. We must all know. I'm sorry I was rude, Raymond. You see, although I quite like you, in spite of what I said—that was the everyday bitching you understand. Men and women are often very unsafe indeed together. Being page to a Lady and her Knight is a strange occupation . . . And, and I just don't trust you.

RAYMOND: You think I trust you? You're too bloody good and clever to live. Making everyone feel so *good* when they're with you. I don't know what they see in you. You're just a fork-tongued, lizardly posh old pouf to me.

GLEN: It's true perhaps; what I know I lacked in humour I tried to make up for in wit.

24

RAYMOND: Thanks for the apology.

GLEN: You were only doing your job. Bearing your errand. Perhaps it's because I find you so ineffably unattractive. It's a fault *we* all share, I'm afraid.

(RAYMOND *goes out and* GLEN *returns to his manuscript.* SALLY *and* BEN *appear from their room. She is carrying* BEN's *package.*)

SALLY: Did you tell him?

RAYMOND: Yes.

SALLY: How'd he take it? Was he sorry?

RAYMOND: I don't know what goes on in his mind. Perhaps he was just thinking of his old book. He was just bitchy to me.

SALLY: Doesn't surprise me. Doesn't know how he's supposed to react with the least intrusion on his comfy academic hibernation. Shirley?

RAYMOND: Very upset. Burst into floods. Stopped painting. Said she'd talk to both of you whenever you'd like her to.

BEN: Christ! Revelations!

SALLY: That's *some*thing. Jo?

RAYMOND: Just going now. She's in the kitchen getting the Professor's whole wheatgerm natural honey and tea.

SALLY: Good. *She*'ll be pleased. Hurry up.

(*He goes.*)

Now I'm going to see what you took the trouble to——

BEN: Don't you think you should try it on in the bedroom?

SALLY: Why? I *know* what it is. I saw it in *Vogue.* I'll just put the top on. Anyway, why shouldn't you buy me a present?

BEN: Well——

SALLY: Well, what?

BEN: It might seem a bit inappropriate. I mean, if we're supposed to be separating.

SALLY: I don't see why. I should still expect you to send me presents. And, if we should go ahead with it, I'll probably send you something quite expensive, like a Sulka dressing-gown or a shirt from Turnbull and Asser. What will you send me?

25

BEN: A bar of carbolic, I should think. Good for the inside of the mouth.

SALLY: You were always unforgiving.

BEN: You need real stamina for the forgiving you've got in mind.

SALLY: Well, you certainly don't have it.

BEN: No, I don't. Oh, try it on.

SALLY: Darling, it's ravishing. Perfect. They're just *in* now.

BEN: Is that Good?

SALLY: Oh, you always want the day before yesterday's fashion. Isn't it Divine? Do you think this is the right colour for me?

BEN: Yes, that's why I chose it.

SALLY: Oh, don't be like that. Do you?

BEN: Well, I can get the other one.

SALLY: No. If you're not interested—No, I've decided this is the one. Darling, thank you, how clever you are . . . What good taste you have.

BEN: Oh, I thought you said my taste in all things was execrable.

SALLY: You're making it up. In women perhaps. Anyway I wouldn't use a pompous word like execrable. *You* sound pretty funny saying it. More like Glen.

(JO *comes in with tea tray.*)

JO: Oh, sorry.

SALLY: Jo—darling—come in. Look what Ben brought me back! Wasn't it clever of him? Just what I wanted.

JO: It's beautiful. You always seem to know where to go for Sally's clothes.

BEN: We have costumiers and wardrobe mistresses in movies, you know. The last movie I made just about paid off the wardrobe. That's all, in fact.

JO: Still—it's spiffing.

SALLY: Colour right, do you think?

JO: Bang on.

SALLY: Ben wasn't sure. This cut's just right for my shoulders. You have to have the shoulders. Hopeless if you're all round. Just make you look gi-normous. Feel it. The stitching.

JO: I certainly will. I'll just take Glen in his tea. He's had no lunch again. Too much work I suppose.

SALLY: I'll wear the whole thing tonight for dinner. All wrong here—but you could about go anywhere in it, couldn't you? I'm so *tired* of all my clothes down here. Same old thing, all the time.

JO: See you in a minute.

(*She goes into* GLEN's *room. Inside she puts down the tray. She feels his forehead, kisses it. Then sits down to watch him sleep.*)

SALLY: Looks as if *she* could do with something new. But I expect you like all that woolly skirt and shawl bit. Perhaps they'll bring back the Dirndl just for you. (*She puts the skirt up to her and watches in the mirror.*)

Fabulous. Ben, you're a miracle.

(*She kisses him.* SHIRLEY *appears at her door at this moment.*)

BEN: Just glad you like it.

SALLY: I'm sorry I said all that. Unforgivable. *Don't* tell me how much it was.

(SHIRLEY *disappears, unseen to them.*)

BEN: They *were* pretty unforgivable.

SALLY: I *have* apologized.

BEN: As the truck said to the corpse. They *were* unforgivable.

SALLY: What else can I do? Why did you give me the bloody outfit then? To make me feel bad? Or just plain old guilt?

BEN: Neither. I've given up guilt many a long Lent ago. And I don't think I'd be able to make *you* feel bad.

SALLY: Just yourself bad? *More* bad.

BEN: They're all past habits.

SALLY: Better than some of your other habits.

BEN: Anyway. I'm glad you liked it.

SALLY: Are you really? Glad?

BEN: If it gives you pleasure.

SALLY: God, you sound pious! You look like some foul-minded stained old monk.

BEN: It might look a bit odd——

SALLY: Odd? You mean I don't look good enough in it?

BEN: You look splendid.

SALLY: You're afraid of what your precious friends will think?

BEN: I mean it's just a bit odd when they've just been told we're splitting up at last.

SALLY: You mean we *are* splitting up?

BEN: *They* think we are.

SALLY: *They* think you're odd enough already.

BEN: But not *you*.

SALLY: At least *I'm* alive.

BEN: Bully for you!

SALLY: You're just a hulk. All right, I *won't* wear it. I'll wear a kaftan and prayer beads and look like one of those virginal young nymphomaniacs. It's pathetic!

BEN: Hear bloody hear! Listening to you is.

SALLY: All you scared, failing, middle-aged men. Memory laneing for young brides, all of you. Nauseating. Why don't you grow up?

BEN: Why don't *you*? Men may become little boys but women never become little girls. It's why they lack the charm of a past life.

SALLY: Oh, good! Sound very appealing to the slavering males from the nose-job and mouth twenty-year-old, twenty-year-old plastic tit and bum dolly in your next carnival of melancholy movie. I can just see it. It's your wallets they're after, diddums, not your paunch, flabby old winkle and profile in depth, sight and sound.

BEN: You're the one who can't face the future.

SALLY: At least I don't mewl over the past, playing pat-a-cake with my past, saying I'm an *artist*.

BEN: I've never called myself an artist and you know it.

SALLY: Well, you *act* the part—very badly, I may say. Heavy performance. (*Yawns*.)

BEN: I've told you, I'm not even second rate. I'm third rate and pretty suspect at that.

SALLY: You're *second* rate. Like degrees at Oxford. Not clever enough to be careless First or imaginative and high-spirited enough to scrape yourself a Third.

BEN: What is today? Curse again? You're the only woman I
    know who has it twenty-eight days a month.
SALLY: Barren, you mean?
BEN: Barren in spirit.
SALLY: The only spirit you'd know comes in two bottles daily.
BEN: Preferable to *your* high spirits. What's so special today
    then, Miss Jackboots?
SALLY: You can't hurt *me*.
BEN: I couldn't. That was the first thing I gave up. Or is it
    the oncoming hot flushes?
SALLY: Take a look at your own face. Flushed with booze and
    your self, your oozing, soggy self. Believe me——
BEN: If men had to go through——
SALLY: It's the *men*-o-pause. All right. Male menopause.
    God, you must have had it along with your acne when
    you were lighter. A pretty sight. Hasn't even cleared up
    now. Pock-marks and veins. *You* gave in years ago. I'm
    just beginning! Whee!
BEN: Good. Clearly suits you.
SALLY: Were you going to say something? What was it? My
    complexion, my hair, my tits? Let me tell you I wear the
    same bra I wore twenty years ago.
BEN: What were you—in the Brigade of Guards?
SALLY: You mean I'm flat chested?
BEN: Flat-headed.
SALLY: I'm not one of your cuddly little armfuls.
BEN: No, you're not. But some people like to embrace
    pythons round their necks.
SALLY: See what they're like when they're thirty: boobs,
    round thighs and arses you could stick a telephone
    directory . . .
BEN: Sense of humour? If not proportion?
SALLY: You're the one with no sense of humour. Except for
    your same old jokes. The only joke you don't see is
    yourself.
BEN: You should have been a writer.
SALLY: You should have been a film director.
BEN: Ta.

SALLY: I *am* a writer.

BEN: Of Broadway comedies?

SALLY: You know—novels.

BEN: Short stories. Listen——

SALLY (*mimics*): 'Listen'.

BEN: I've thrown better writers than you off TV commercials. *Men* writers. You need more than a resentful memory to be a writer.

SALLY: Oh, what do you know about it.

BEN: Then don't wear the bloody thing!
(*He snatches the new outfit from her and flings it right across the room. She looks at him calmly and then goes and picks them up, folding them and carefully packing them back in the box.*)

SALLY: If you're trying to attempt impressive gestures, remember that largeness demands needle control. That's why they upset you when they say your pictures are formless, self-indulgent and undisciplined.
(*Presently, he goes to her.*)
Anyway, it's a size too large.

BEN: No. I checked.

SALLY: You *checked*! Oh, yes, right for once . . .

BEN: Do wear it this evening.

SALLY: I'm going out this evening.

BEN: Who with?

SALLY: I don't know yet. No one round here. Shirley. No, she'll be all heavy lidded about our tragic separation. That and some new set of refugees.

BEN: Oh, Raymond. Of course . . .

SALLY: I might. There *is* that nice young farmer who rides so beautifully. *He* keeps ringing.

BEN: *Does* he?

SALLY: *He* didn't come from the back streets of Swansea to settle in Hammersmith. He *knows* a bit of class.

BEN: Ah, we revert! So, the Country Lifers really are Britain's spinal cord, after all.

SALLY: Some spine with a little wine would be fine. Can't face another homespun dinner with you lot.

BEN: Leaving me to it, eh?

SALLY: You'll cope. Think how sorry they'll be for you. Left all alone . . .

BEN: Sally, *I'm* sorry——

SALLY: No, you're not. You just *lost*.
(*He goes to touch her.*)
You've begun to smell . . .
(RAYMOND *enters with tea tray.*)
Physically. I can smell you in bed. And now in here . . . Mum's tea?
(RAYMOND *nods.*)
Let him take it up to her himself.

RAYMOND: No. It's all right. I've got it now.
(*He proceeds upstairs.*)

SALLY: He's afraid to go himself. And lazy. Can't stand the sight of her. Not surprised. Tell her to put her teeth in if she ever comes down. Not that she will. Still, you can understand—like, where he gets *his* narrow, squinny eyes from. Oh, no, the old man had those too. Very Welsh that. At least he's not proud of *that*. Dinner out somewhere, dolly, Raymond. We could have a bit of a dance or something.

RAYMOND: Sure. But what about——

SALLY: The Refectory Party can amuse themselves tonight. We might even dress up and go to London. Would you hate it, Ben? Your wife with a pouf? After all, I'm leaving you with *yours*. Only he's more distinguished than mine.

BEN: Suit yourself. You *will* . . .
(RAYMOND *disappears. Pause.*)
I brought you your weeklies and magazines, and books you asked for.

SALLY: Thanks.

BEN: Thanks for the thanks.
(RAYMOND *reappears.*)

SALLY: How is the old crone?

RAYMOND: O.K. Feeding the cats. She's having a tray in her room as usual.

SALLY (*to* BEN): Job for you—*son.*

C   31

BEN (*sings*):

> 'At seventeen he fell in love quite madly
> With eyes of a tender blue,
> At twenty-four . . .'

SALLY: 'He groaned along once more'.
Can't you shut up?

BEN: No. Can you?

> 'At thirty-five he . . .'

SALLY: 'He's still alive . . .'

BEN: Di di da—di da, etc.

> 'But it's when he thinks he's past love——'

SALLY: He *is*.

(*They sing together.*)

SALLY
BEN } : 'And he loves her as *he's never loved before*.'

SALLY: And bully for him! Couldn't have been much cop at seventeen. As for *past* love. Poor girl!

BEN: I don't know. Might have a civilizing influence on her.

RAYMOND: I'll go and start some of the dinner. Vegetables . . .

SALLY: Why should you? Let Jo do it. She's the young lady who lives in a shoe.

(RAYMOND *goes out quickly.*)

BEN: They do say——

SALLY: They? Who's they?

BEN: They—the people *you* like to read in those magazines, showing off about the novels they've read, film, plays, and poetry. They, they say some people live their art while others merely create it. When are you going to write yours out?

SALLY: When I'm good and ready. Pretty soon.

BEN: I'm sure they'll all recognize your portrait.

SALLY: What? Of *you*. Are you joking? Who do you think wants to recognize a portrait of *you*? I should cut out on the hard stuff and just tipple with your own spirits. Best for you. I've better things to write about . . .
(*Pause.*)

BEN: Are you really going out with Raymond?

SALLY: Yes.

BEN: Right, well piss off then.

SALLY: I shall. I'm reading.

BEN: Reading. Writing books. Books. The world's a battle-field. No, a sewage farm of books. Look at them all. Written for people like you.

SALLY: And Glen.

BEN: At least they're good.

SALLY: A bubble. Of literary luminaries. Books about people who wrote books, painted pictures, made films—you said yourself we were choking ourselves to death with the effluent of celluloid.

BEN: I did. I try not to add to it.

SALLY: Don't worry. You will. As long as it gets flushed away . . .

(*Pause.*)

You'll have Shirley to comfort you and tell her how different she is from her sister.

BEN: She sure is.

SALLY: Will you tell her how much you despise her paltry middle-class Marxist daubings and her nanny-derived Maoist marches in Grosvenor Square and Hyde Park?

BEN: I already have. You remember quite well. She burst into tears in your room.

SALLY: The next time?

BEN: She laughed and said I was an old silly who didn't know what was going on.

SALLY: Bright girl!

BEN: Well, I told the truth. That's one thing I haven't learned to do with you.

(*Pause.*)

SALLY: I'm tired of this; Raymond!

(RAYMOND *comes in.*)

Let's take his Lordship's dog out for him. He'll never take her out himself and *he* wanted to film Francis of Assisi! Can you imagine: my little brothers and sisters!

RAYMOND: I'll get my wellies. It's wet.

SALLY: O.K. I'll get mine. Fresh air's what we need.

(*They go to their respective rooms.* BEN *hesitates and then*

33

goes to the telephone, which he dials.)

BEN (*phone*): Hullo. Chivers Hotel? May I speak to Mrs.
Marion Silcox? Yes . . . Tell her it's Mr. Prosser.
PROSSER. That's right . . .
(*Both* SALLY *and* RAYMOND *reappear, clad in macintosh
and wellingtons, dog's lead, etc.*)
(*As Sally descends stairs.*)
Hullo, Marion? Yes. It is . . . Ben. Look. I'm not going,
I say, I'm not going to talk for long . . . No, I don't
want to talk to her. I want to talk to you. Will you come
down? Yes, I know I said not. And I don't want the
child damaged. I say—I say we can all be *over* protected.
Yes, if we don't watch it. Yes. I know that's my fault. I
wanted the minimum of bloodshed . . . And, of, yes, of
course, the result was carnage all round. But as you said.
Why *shouldn't* we meet. We've been, well, years. Keep
the child in the hotel . . . Well, sort of separated . . .
You know what *she's* like. Everyone's like. Hanging on,
yes. What? No, please come . . . Oh, I don't know. Any
time when you can. I ask you—*I'll* be here. I'm tired of
being told *what* I want to do, *who* I should see. Promise?
Oh, it'll be ugly. What else? What's left us that isn't ugly?
Ring me when you get here. It'll be all right.
(SALLY *snatches the phone from him as he struggles to keep
it away.*)

SALLY: Marion? Oh, yes, your strangled voice . . . This is
Sally. Yes, your ex-husband's wife. Do come down if
your runty little legs will stand. Bring the brat. No one
will harm her. Certainly not me. I wouldn't touch her.
And, oh yes, fuck him if you like. In my bed. I doubt if
I shall be here to watch the spectacle. But there will be
others. Goodbye . . .
(*She puts down the receiver and goes to the main door.*)
Got the lead, Raymond? We might take her in the car
for a bit.
(*She stands at the door.* RAYMOND *follows. Slowly,* BEN
*opens the gift box. He takes out the new outfit and
unwrapping it slowly tears it into shreds. In front of them.*

34

Systematically he throws them outside. Including the box.)
SALLY (*presently*): Time for walkies.
BEN (*to* RAYMOND): You wormy——
RAYMOND: Faggot?
SALLY: You shouldn't have thrown the box on the rails. The line isn't yours yet you know!
(*They go out.* BEN *hurls some tissue paper after them and closes the door.* SHIRLEY *watches from her door and comes down. She gets him a drink and leads him to a sofa. Presently, she kisses him.*)
BEN: You've always discouraged me before.
SHIRLEY: Events change. Time strikes . . . I'll leave you. No, I'm *not* going to discuss Sally. That doesn't mean I might not go to bed with you . . . Now I think I'll go up and get the rest of the light . . . I know what you think of me. But perhaps you all think too much of personal relationships. One, two, three, four . . .
(*She starts to go back to her room.*)
By the way, I'm not some malleable side of her coin—or anyone else's.
(*She goes out, leaving him alone. In the other main room,* GLEN *has awoken uneasily.* JO *goes to him.*)
JO: Darling.
GLEN: Jo. You're here.
JO: I'm here. How are you feeling?
GLEN: There was a lot of shouting. Noise. Voices. In other rooms. All gone. All gone.
JO: Glen, you've not eaten again. Why won't you see the doctor?
GLEN: Later. Later.
JO: Later. It's always later. You've finished your book.
GLEN: Yes. Isn't it a relief. I think I feel hungry enough for one of your dinners.
JO: I read it, well, the last of it, while you were sleeping. My dear heart, I love you. I dread to wake up and you not there.
GLEN: There are other voices. Other places. You don't need mine.

JO: I do. I do. You are what I care for. The thing that's left. Not fleeing away. I read your letters. You are in my brain, not just my heart. Even in my bed with others. I need your rebuke. Your smile when I'm naughty or stupid and misunderstanding. You've lit my silly school-girl life. You've brought me up. Slapped life into me. Don't let me get old. Not when you are still so young. I'm sorry. I can't bear to be alone. For I *will* be. The rest means so little, without you. My reading and silly letters and walks with you and rides and my awful home-weave cooking . . .

GLEN: Go and do some more.

JO: Tell me more. Your love, yes, the boys, the desolation, even the *fame*. Keep your clothes with mine here and your things. And my heart in yours.

GLEN: It's there, my dearest. It *is* there. Always.

JO: Your spectacles. I've broken them . . .

GLEN: Ben and Sally have broken up.

JO: Yes. I know. Stay there. I'll be back.
    (*She goes out, nodding at* BEN.)
    Could I have a drink? I've just got to make a call.

BEN: Sure.
    (*He gets one.*)

JO: Hullo, Dr. Ashton? Sorry to bother you, but yes; I think he's getting worse. I know he should. But perhaps if you come again? He's finished his book . . . His . . . Well, anyway, if you could. When you've time. No. Not *immediate*. 'Bye.

BEN: Worse?

JO: Yes.

BEN: How rotten.

JO: He seems better.

BEN: Which is a bad sign.

JO: Yes . . . I'm sorry about——

BEN: Oh, well. End of a long tunnel for all.

JO: I won't ask you any details. I must prepare the dinner.

BEN: I'll help you.

JO: How was your little girl?

36

BEN: Oh. It's nice to hear it *uninflected*. I don't know. What
do I know about little girls? Or anyone, for that. Someone asked me once what I think of 'young people' and
I was more or less pilloried for it. How many or how
much do *I* know. When I was a little boy, I didn't know
much about other little boys. Except I didn't like them
over much. Nor them me. Little girls, some yes, a lot.

JO: How was she?

BEN: Can I say this? Well, I will, on the way to, to: fierce,
proud and gentle.

JO: Don't let them persuade you she doesn't love you. Even
if she doesn't love you now—she, oh she will.

BEN: Hard to love a renegade father.

JO: You're not *my* renegade father. And *I* love you.

BEN: You love so many people.

JO: I know. You *suspect* it.

BEN: No. Like a believer, I *doubt*. You love Glen.

JO: Yes.

BEN: You can't think of life without him?

JO: No.

BEN: And me?

JO: Yes.

BEN: Why do you love me? I see why you love Glen.

JO: I love you because I *am* love for you. I am your child,
your protector. Oh, doesn't it sound twee?

BEN: Yes. But TWUE.

JO: I am the seed in your earth. I shine on upon you and you
are there always . . . Ben, perhaps not . . .
(*Pause.*)

BEN: I was the, well the protagonist of the most degrading
spectacle. Today.

JO: Tell me.

BEN: May I? There's no one . . . I'll cut it right down. I was
sitting in the restaurant with my daughter. She refused
a cushion for her chair like she used to have. Very
politely. I looked at her. She looked at me. I talked
about the restaurant, the waiter, the food, who went
there, what dishes there were. She ordered promptly,

37

courteously. She tackled her spaghetti, her steak, her ice cream. Her coke. We said less and less. I wanted her to go. *She* wanted to go. To be with her friends, her mother, I don't know who. I drank an extra half litre of wine. I ordered the wine. Got the bill in a hurry. I looked at her, and, well, yes the awful, the thing is I cried all over the tablecloth. In front of her. She watched my jowls move. I looked away. But I couldn't. Through the marble and columns and the rest of the silencing restaurant and waiters scrupulously *not* watching. I couldn't even get out 'Let's go'. Then, suddenly, she leapt off her too low chair and put her arms round me. And *she* cried. Like a 'B' movie. She took my hand and we walked out past all the rows of tables. I left her at home and we neither of us said a word; just held hands; no, she knew the way home. Isn't that despicable? How could I face her? That's why I rang . . . I dare say . . .

(*Pause.*)

JO: We'll be such friends and lovers and not mind being sentimental or even romantic if we can manage.

BEN: We have been.

JO: What?

BEN: Friends and Lovers.

JO: Yes. But we shall grow from a new childhood. I shall crave for you and you'll quicken for me. Even if there are others.

BEN: Does Glen know?

JO: Yes. He delights in it. It will be all right. That of it as— —*that*! It. Is. Now. Will be. Has been. We *are*! We'll never really leave. Even if we get on our nerves. Oh, Ben, I'm frightened! But I'm all right. Kiss me . . . And later. All the rest and the rest and the rest . . .

(*They embrace.*)

There's Glenny. Come in, my darling. We're so happy suddenly, we've been kissing and cuddling and your book's finished and we're going to have roast lamb and peas from the garden and that claret of yours.

(*He is inside the room.*)

GLEN: Oh, my dear both.

(*He embraces them both.* SHIRLEY *enters.*)

SHIRLEY (*entering*): All right then.

JO: Shirley, Glen's finished his book. I love him. I can't bear to go into his room. I love Ben, no, you think I'm light-minded, a lot of people do. Like they think about you. I think and welcome you within all I know up to this now, this moment, with my heart full and my brain clear and empty. Forgive me for what I am not. But I am—I am a loving creature . . . I'm frail and I break but bear with me . . . It's hard to love, isn't it? It's like religion without pain, I mean it's not religion *without* pain. It's not flowers and light and fellowship. It's cruel and we inhabit each other's dark places. Let's drink to that. It's not much worse than the rest. The time is short and all our heads are sore and our hearts sick oh, into the world, this century we've been born into and made and been made by. Release us from ourselves and give us each our other. There: I've said, I've invented a grace, not very gracefully. Oh, Glen, bless you, the life you've given me, at least, and you Ben, for the work and pain you long to exorcise, and you Shirley for being such a butt with such human grace. Damn it, I didn't mean to cry. How indecent.

BEN: It's been an indecent sort of day.

JO: Well, it won't be. We'll all have dinner and talk and think of love, even if there are lumps of hate within us. Please say yes. There isn't long.

GLEN: No. You're right. Say it while you can. Naively, if you like. While you can. There will be no counting, cant or otherwise. Cant on Unchristian Soldiers.

SHIRLEY: Are we drunk already?

GLEN: No. And what would it matter. I have . . . tried to love. No, I *have* loved. I love Jo. I love you (*to* BEN) and the rest of you.

SHIRLEY: We *are* drunk already.

BEN: No. We're not! We *will* be but we're not. It's too late to persist in our folly.

GLEN: Or to become wise.

BEN: Oh, come, you're wise. You're very wise.

GLEN: No I'm not. I took to writing about people in recent times because I thought it might show us what we are yesterday and today. They're starting to wonder. But too late. My book's no good. It's too late. The century pulled the carpet out from me. Cleverness and all.

BEN: My films are not much. What does it matter? Her paintings are no good and her protests are a terribly real joke on us all. Her (JO's) love is no good. How can you be a romantic in a world that despises imagination and only gives instruction in orgasms? The response and admiration of virtues. Where? Now. It's not in the crushing of the worm of will. The imagination.

GLEN: The cast worm forgives the plough.

BEN: Oh, shut up, my dead darling.

GLEN: Strive, no, arrive at detachment.

BEN: I wish I had. Strive for apathy. Hope and fear. Members of one another.

JO: We're a rag bag. A glorious, silly old rag bag!

BEN: Providence, duty, the sufficiency of virtue.

SHIRLEY: You *are* stoned.

BEN: No. Noiseless terror.

GLEN: English Catholicism was different, but it saw that the whole future was to be decided by the sheer amount of its noise.

SHIRLEY: Anyone hungry yet?

BEN: What will it be *like?* It hasn't begun to *work*. Us. The Twentieth Century. You (*To* SHIRLEY) hate us. Why do they hate us. They'll be worse off. More frightened, more huddling for comfort. They do it now. Thin and careless like none of us had ever been. Precept: be bold. There will never be more perfection than there is now. Glen and Jo are together. Shall we lie in bed?

SHIRLEY: No.

BEN: Quite right. Improper. Suggestion. Anyway, I lust for Jo. What *will* it be like. Time future. Now, this is, this is saloon bar. Bar talk. Do you know the worst cut they made

40

on the road?

GLEN: I can think of several.

BEN: My God, my God, why has Thou forsaken me?

GLEN: Not bad.

SHIRLEY: My God—you sicken me.

BEN: Good. That was my patent intention.

GLEN: I *did* always delight in the Absurd. But where is it *gone*?

BEN: Bullies. Bullies who tell you what to do and think. Like Shirley. Do you know the Edwardians must have been the last to have known that *their* appearance—at the expense of others, mark, gave pleasure to others.

GLEN: I was the last of them, about.

BEN: Age cant. Past. Present. Futurology. Now, how do you get to be a futurologist?

JO: Take a Master's degree.

BEN: The *Way* it *will* be. Is. Not long to go. Glenny, my darling, end-of-term one. Kiss me.
  (*They embrace.*)

BEN: May I kiss Jo?
  (*He does so. Passionately.*)
  (*GLEN watches in a, yes, exquisite desolation.*)
  Ah, the old, silent life of England, eh Shirley?

SHIRLEY: And good riddance.

BEN: You do all right out of the residue of it. Seeing revolutionary worlds in a grain of sand, eh, chucky, chucky.

GLEN: *I* never liked the judicial tone . . .

BEN: Oh, it will totter on. Glen will write about the twentieth century and the people who lived it. Shirley will paint and barricade. Jo will take lovers. I will grow old in films . . . Oh God . . . this is a loveless place.
  (*The main door opens.* SALLY *and* RAYMOND *appear. She is carrying the dead wet body of a largish dog. She moves into the room. Presently*:)

SALLY: They shot her. She was on heat and we stupidly let her fly off miles away. We saw them from the top of the hill, helpless. They tied, yes tied her to a tree and set all the

41

male dogs on her. And then they shot her . . . In front of us.

SHIRLEY: Oh God.

SALLY: Pigs, all of you. Why don't you ring the vet?

RAYMOND: She's dead, darling.

SALLY: Here she is. *Your*. Your dog.

(*She staggers upstairs.* RAYMOND *takes the animal's body from* BEN.)

RAYMOND: I'll take her.

(BEN *rushes after her, up the stairs. She turns.*)

SALLY: *Your* dog!

(*He goes to put an arm round her. She hits him in the face. He staggers, recovers and they begin hitting each other. The rail breaks and she falls to the ground.*)

You've broken my back!

BEN: Good!

(*He jumps down. Almost on top of her.*)

It was *my* dog. And *you've* broken *my* back.

SALLY: Do something, someone. Let something *happen*!

BEN: Keep away. I'll kill her! I'll kill her! She's killed *me*. She's killed *everything*. Long ago.

SALLY: I haven't. But I would. And somebody will!

(*He smashes her in the face, and they kick and tear at each other, clothes tearing and splitting. Blood and breakage. The others watch them fight while* RAYMOND *holds the dead dog in his arms.*)

CURTAIN

act two

The following day. Same set. JO *is sitting alone in the main set.* GLEN *is lying in his room, watched over by* BEN. SALLY *comes down the stairs.*

JO: I've made some tea. Good British custom after the blitz.
SALLY: Is the Doctor here yet?
JO: No. Don't fret.
SALLY: I am.
JO: Of course.
SALLY: You think he's dying?
JO: Of course. For ages. What's left? Now?
SALLY: Indeed. I think my jaw's broken.
JO: Oh, my dear.
SALLY: I don't think it matters much. Do you? What isn't broken? Dead? Disappearing?
JO: Oh, Sally. Don't.
SALLY: What?
JO: Split: up.
SALLY: That doesn't seem to matter much either. It's there. But it's gone. Another horseless carriage.
JO: I love you both.
SALLY: You love Ben?
JO: Yes.
SALLY: And Glen?
JO: Glen is the life. If he goes. It all. Goes. Gone. The wit, the irony, the kindness, the struggle with himself which he never unburdened.
SALLY: No. He didn't do that . . .

43

JO: He was a *friend*, Sally. A man of friendship. He clove to
your silliness and never betrayed you. People said he was
a bitch but he wasn't.

SALLY: Isn't.

JO: He had high standards but he kept them for himself. He
didn't admire what he was, which was a great deal, but
admired a lot of the others. I broke his spectacles . . . I
can't bear the room without him. His forehead. His
breathing. His arcane jokes and odd fancies. I love his old
clothes. His letters and his bad drawings. His restless
indolence. His sickly athleticism. His tolerance and
forbearing. Oh, I'm going on as if he's dead. But he's
breathing heavily in my heart, more than he ever did. Oh,
Glen, my brilliant, kindly, silly Glen. You listened to my
chirruping and ate my home-made jam which you didn't
like. Your frail, fastidious, greedy body, loving, full of
lust and circumspection . . . He was ashamed of his boys,
you know. No, not ashamed of them but himself, his own
odd body and over-turning mind. He would listen to my
affairs with men, my daft letters and exchange drawings,
make jokes I didn't understand and didn't mind. He
loved me, he *did*, didn't he?

SALLY: He did. The best of a poor world for you both . . . Do
you love me?

JO: Yes. I always have.

SALLY: Like you love Ben?

JO: Oh, same only different. You know . . .

SALLY: Because I've got to love you. Gotten, as the
Americans say. You rouse my inside with—with—your
caprice, your enthusiasm, your odd, withdrawn moods.
Your strong, thriving body, your sturdy legs and hard
arms, I——

JO: Yes?

SALLY: No. Glen's in your being now.

JO: You can't drive that out.

SALLY: No.

JO: Do you want to make love to me?

SALLY: Yes. I want to kiss you. On the mouth. My tongue

44

between your bright teeth. I want to hold you in my
arms a whole night with our bodies like twin fortresses,
lap in lap. I want to see you wake up and look down at
me and get me awake . . . May I kiss you?

JO: As long as you want. *I* want you to.

(*They kiss, gently, forcibly.*)

SALLY: They'd call us a couple of old diesels.

JO: Who cares? Glen wouldn't.

SALLY: Jo . . . Let's go away. When it's all over. And you
think you can and still want to. I know it's not the time
but, yes, it *is* the time. Because it's running out, and we
should be running away, running away together where
we see fit or fine . . . I really do love you. *I'm tired of the
bodies of men.* They've gone through my life and I'm just
like a, oh, closed line, service discontinued. We could go
on for as long as we like. Oh, Jo, I want to hold you and
cuddle you and rest in your body . . .

JO: My darling.

(*They kiss again.*)

SALLY: Oh, your body. The next few weeks, months will be
foul. But be patient. I've tried to learn. Give us a chance.
No one else will. We'll dress in what we want, go where
we like, think of each other as well as the rest. You are
so—near. Dear. Don't let this chance slide. It won't
occur again. Other lines aren't the same.

JO: What about Ben?

SALLY: Ben thinks he needs me. *I* thought so. But he'll be so
relieved. Especially if it's you and me. He might even
make a film out of it. Promise! Say promise! No. Don't
say. Just nod . . .

(JO *nods. They embrace.*)

JO: People laugh at this sort of thing. Like Poor Glen.

SALLY (*mad!*): Well, Ben wouldn't do that.

JO: Is Ben——

SALLY: Oh, I've stupidly told him he is. And he's always
wandering—naturally. But I don't think so. He's a
wanderer. Stay at home nomad, rather.

JO: Sally?

SALLY: Jo . . .

JO: Sally . . .

SALLY: Jo. Oh, Jo, joke, Sally of *OUR* alley. I love you in a hundred ways and I won't look up one anthology to tell you how. Strange. I wanted to love my sister. But I didn't. Ben wanted to love his sister—like an extra wife to carry the burden. But she died. And left him with me. Oh, and Marion. His father. His mother. And his daughter. Thank heavens *we'll* have no children, Jo. Jo and Sally—our own offspring. Hold me again. No man's held me like that since I can't remember.

(*Door bell rings.*)

Now let's wipe our eyes. That'll be the doctor. It'll be hard, Jo. But don't forget this when you're going through it all. It'll still be there when it's time. Glen would like it.

JO: Shall I tell him?

SALLY: Up to you.

(SALLY *goes to the front door and ushers in* DR. ASHTON.)

Good morning, Dr. Ashton. Thanks for coming so soon.

ASHTON: Nasty cut and bruise on your face. All right, are you?

SALLY: Oh yes, rural life. You know.

ASHTON: How's the patient?

SALLY: You *said* it. Worse.

ASHTON: I'm not surprised. I told Miss—er—here months ago. Hospital was the place.

SALLY: Not a railway station.

ASHTON: This is the way, isn't it? Booking hall?

JO: Shall I come?

ASHTON: If you wish. Perhaps not.

(*She follows him into the room.* BEN *goes out. She follows him as the* DOCTOR *examines him.* SALLY *goes upstairs, leaving* BEN *and* JO *alone. He grasps her hand, which she takes uncertainly.*)

BEN: All right?

JO: No . . . Scared.

BEN: Don't be. Sally?

JO: She's fine. She says you've broken her jaw.

BEN: I couldn't break a sparrow's jaw.
   (*Pause.*)
   Jo, I do love you.
JO: I know.
BEN: And you?
JO: Yes.
BEN: We could sift something out of the rubble. I want to
   hold you. Now, I'm afraid.
JO: I know. So do I. But Glen's dying in there. That's where
   I should be now.
   (*She goes into* GLEN's *room. The* DOCTOR *is already leaving
   and moves to the main set.*)
ASHTON: I don't like to move him but I'll get him into the
   cottage hospital straight away. It's early (*looks at watch*)—
   as soon as I can.
JO: Cottage hospital! Can't you get him to London?
ASHTON: I doubt if he'd make it. Sorry. I'll be back. Soon as
   I can.
SALLY: Doctor Ashton—is it——
ASHTON: Yes. I'm afraid it is. Very soon. I'll find my way
   across the platform. I'm sorry.
   (*He goes.* JO *lets out a great howl and hurls herself into the
   other room on to* GLEN's *still figure. Pause.*)
BEN: Oh, well.
SALLY: Well, what?
   (RAYMOND *and* SHIRLEY *have appeared.*)
BEN: It's Glen. Er, Jo. He's for the chopper. Right away.
SALLY: Right away? Well, what?
BEN: Well, we all have to go sometime, as my old mother
   used to say.
SALLY: I wish *she'd* go! Have you taken her cupper tea up to
   her yet? Well, I will. And I'll smash her face in with it.
   Like you did mine. See what you did.
BEN: Beautiful bone structure unaltered.
SALLY: If you were a man——
BEN: I've never claimed so much. Perhaps *you* should. Your
   upper cut's better than mine. *And* your feet and knees.
SALLY: If you had any balls, I'd have kicked them into the

siding.

BEN: Still British Railways property. Till the end of the month. All right are we all then?

SALLY: I'm going for a walk. Jo, come for a walk. Ben'll stay —if he can.

BEN: Yes. I will.

(JO *appears at the door*.)

JO: He did love me. His eyes are so blue—and he held my hand so tight it hurt.

SALLY: Come for a walk.

JO: No. I'll wait. On the platform. The sun's up now. It's warm.

(SALLY *clasps her. She closes the door*.)

SALLY: Right. Walkies. Till the Doc returns.

RAYMOND: I think I'll stay in case I'm needed.

SALLY: O.K. Shirley?

SHIRLEY: Right. Bit of exercise.

BEN: Bit of exercise!

SALLY: Shut up, you!

BEN: And you shut up, fat-mouth. A friend's dying in there.

SALLY: No friend of yours. Come on, Shirley. (*To* JO.) Raymond will get you anything you want. Gormless won't.

JO: Thanks. I'll just wait.

(SALLY *and* SHIRLEY *go out*.)

SALLY: Wish *I* had a shotgun today.

(*Exit*.)

JO: I'll just sit outside I think. It's quite warm.

(BEN *embraces her*.)

BEN: Just wait. It's ridiculous to say it. But wait. Get drunk. Sleep. It will pass. I want you . . . I shouldn't have said that.

JO: Why not? If you mean it. Glen would be pleased. Oh, Glen.

BEN: There . . .

JO: Glen come back. I can't live—with all this. Who can? *You* couldn't even. Do we give up . . .

(*She disengages herself from* BEN.)

Sorry. I'll sit in the sun till the doctor comes back.

BEN: Be careful.

JO: Of what?

BEN: Oh, pedestrian traffic.

(*He sits alone after she's gone out.* RAYMOND *comes in from the kitchen.*)

RAYMOND: Thought I'd bury the dog while they're all out.

BEN: Thoughtful.

RAYMOND: Do you want anything? Coffee?

BEN: No thanks, Raymond. I've got some on.

RAYMOND: Well, I think I'll look in on him. While I have my coffee. They're all out. Except Mum. Why don't you get some sleep?

BEN: Right. Thanks.

RAYMOND: I'll look out for the doctor. Where's Jo?

BEN: Outside. In the platform sun.

RAYMOND: See you then.

BEN: See you.

(RAYMOND *goes.*)

I hope not. Oh . . .

(*He settles into the sofa. In the other room,* RAYMOND *hovers over* GLEN.)

RAYMOND: Glen?

GLEN: Ah . . . Raymond. What is it you've got to tell me? Doctor not here, I hope. Hope he's too late again, that one.

RAYMOND: Can I——

GLEN: I can hear you, you——

RAYMOND: Faggot.

GLEN: Faggots were not so long ago what the working classes used to eat. With peas, I think. And saveloys.

RAYMOND: How would you know?

GLEN: Guardsman told me.

RAYMOND: You bet.

GLEN: Tell me something. If you will.

RAYMOND: What?

GLEN: Were they really separating? Sally and Ben?

RAYMOND: No. Least, not at the time. It was like they wanted you all to decide for them.

49

GLEN: What a disgusting notion. Whose idea was it?

RAYMOND: Hers, I think, but he went along with it in the end. Didn't know what they were doing, either of them.

GLEN: Quite. But to use your friends and *test* them—it's like vivisection on friendship.

RAYMOND: Depends how you feel. I don't think she went much on you.

GLEN: I know. But I admired her. Made more, far more than there was of herself. Well, thanks for telling me. Try not to tell the others. If you can. Especially Jo.

RAYMOND: Well, it's all over bar the shouting, isn't it? I don't mean you, with, well, respect. But what's left in it for any of us?

GLEN: Well, if this is terminal care I can't say I think much
 . of it.

RAYMOND: Doctor'll be here soon.

GLEN: To hell with the Doctor. Where's Jo?

RAYMOND: Sunning herself on the platform with the weighing machines. She's all right. I'll wait here till she comes back. Right?

GLEN: Just as you like . . . I saw two signs on the road coming down. One was a little triangle of green with a hedge and a bench. And a sign read: 'This is a temporary open space' . . .

RAYMOND: Oh yes?

GLEN: And the other was a site of rubble near the Crystal Palace I think, perched high up over London, where the bank managers and cashiers fled at the beginning of our —our—of our century. It said 'Blenkinsop—Demolitionists. We *do* it. You *watch* it. *Come down.*' (*He recedes from consciousness and* RAYMOND *reads a magazine with his coffee at the bedside. The door of the main set opens and* MARION *enters. She is expensively dressed in a tight-fitting fur coat. Slightly younger than* BEN.)

MARION: Darling!

BEN: Marion!

MARION: Ben!

(*They embrace.*)

Are you all alone?

BEN: Sally and Shirley have gone for a walk. The dog's died.

MARION: Oh, darling, you loved that dog.

BEN: Yes, but nobody believed it. Like they don't believe I love our child. Anyone.

MARION: I do. And she does.

BEN: Raymond is in the next room watching over poor darling old Glen—dying fast.

MARION: God!

BEN: And Jo is ice cold in the morning sun outside.

MARION: That must have been the girl I saw on the platform. Like, well, rather like Sally.

BEN: That's the one.

MARION: The one you wanted to have because——

BEN: They were sisters? That was someone else. Marion. That's no thing at all. Why has it got all so bad, so brutish, so devilish, so sneering?

MARION: Calm down, darling. Shall I get you some coffee? Or a drink at this good, early hour.

BEN: Oh, your voice is so *easy*. Just hold on to me. And talk. First: information.

MARION: Well, at first I was utterly bewildered. I *know* you'd had a bad time with the offspring. Though she didn't say a word. She loves you.

BEN: Why? What for.

MARION: She's yours. She likes you. She admires you.

BEN: For what? Being a renegade father's no great shakes. You, know, you know Sally's made me sound like a Hollywood movie. Me! I turned down three million, no five plus a percentage, dollars not to. I'm English I said —what's that any more—I *live* here and I don't want your filthy dollars and broken impulses . . . You look rather lovely at this time of the day.

MARION: I don't. And neither do you. But I can see why. Anyway, when Sally hawked her usual bile down the phone, I wasn't sure what to do. I wasn't going to bring our fledgling, in spite of what you said. Broken noses and

obscenities are just about enough for you and me. But,
no, I left *her* at the hotel with the nanny. But I *had* to
see you. And I don't care about the broken bottles and
flick knives. It's all violent and we've got to find a way
out of it. I'm so sorry about Glen. Is it?

BEN: Yes. Any old time I'd say. Raymond or Jo or Sally will
keep us informed.

MARION: He loved you, Ben.

BEN: Did he, Marion? I don't know anything about all of that
any more. I think he loved me once. I loved him. Oh, I
did. They all thought *I* was a pouf. But I loved him. I
loved him because, because he was him and he made his
own life out of the twentieth century and what a bad one
it was. The century, I mean. But he didn't trim, he didn't
deceive himself, he preened his perverse English
personality and grinned at everyone, and made them feel
better, things more likely to happen but not matter
anyway. He loved and was loved. And in spite of fearing
both of it. I am neither loved nor loving . . . Except I
want *you* at this moment.

MARION: Ben, let's go. I've the car outside. We *can* do it.

BEN: Maybe we can. But not now. I can't leave Glen. To that
bleeding Raymond. And Sally and Shirley. Jo, well she's
different.

MARION: *You* love her?

BEN: In a way. She's a loving thing from an unknown attic.
Take your clothes off. I want you.

MARION: Certainly not. I want *you*. But I do have to drive
back. And I don't really fancy being caught by Jackboots
Sally.

BEN: I shouldn't have said that to you.

MARION: You shouldn't have said a lot of things. Did you tell
her we went to bed yesterday?

BEN: She assumed it, anyway. So, I, I reserved my position.
Fat lot of good it did too. Nearly got killed. She's so
strong. And I'm out well, well out of condition.

MARION: Ben, I know you. Do believe me. You wake up. You
know how. Not 'about' anything. It's just black and

fearsome and impossible to get up. Sweat and loathing.
All too early. You can't read or concentrate or remember.
You sleep endlessly between good or bad times. It's all
the same. We've become islands at the edges of the bed.
You're on your own. I'm on *my* own. Now, for years.
Oh, Ben, it's been a glass steel wall. Both observing the
child and her us. We do—did nothing with her—or her
with us. I tried keeping her out of the bedroom, for my sake
as much as yours. We never did things at the same time
of day. We couldn't. I followed you like a dog when I
knew you wanted to be left alone. You wanted to sleep
in front of the television.

BEN: I know: it's true. You read about it in the papers: 'A
Wife's Problems'. 'How I won through. Why did he
want so desperately to be alone!' Stupid nit. We did love
each other. Dearly. But it was all risk, risk, damned risk,
Gambling. Russian roulette.

MARION: We had our moments, oh, who cares, our moments
of happiness? Months of happiness. Penniless and odd
but relaxing, forgetful happiness.

BEN: We did. You helped. We helped. You see: the more
pain I FEEL, the more resentment comes out of *her*.

MARION: Come back, Ben. Do, do come, Ben. I'll tell you
everything that's happened and you can tell me
everything that's happened. And we'll go through what's
happened with us. It wasn't half bad . . .

BEN: No. It wasn't . . .

MARION: We should have trusted each other then. Instead of
going our ways. Blindly. Hoping. You can't *hope* any
longer. Oh, Ben, come *now*. Before they all come back
and *she* starts smashing the place up. And *I* get scared
and run. And you give up . . . Let's go now. Give
ourselves a chance. Glen wouldn't mind . . . Neither
would Jo.

BEN: Give me time, Marion. Darling.

MARION: There's been a lot of time. A wasteland of it. For all
of us. I think I'll go for a walk and then I'll get into the
car and drive back to London. It's in the old car park.

With a couple of others. I'll wait half an hour.

(*As she gets up to go,* SALLY *and* SHIRLEY *appear at the door.*)

I'm sorry to be so early. I'm just going.

(SALLY *says nothing. Nor* SHIRLEY. BEN *sees her out uneasily.*)

SALLY: Well, did you fuck her?

BEN: Oh, shut up, pig mouth. He's *dying* in there.

SALLY: Were you waiting till he was cold?

BEN: What else do you think of?

SALLY: Plenty. How's Glen?

BEN: Ask Raymond.

SALLY: Raymond! How's Glen?

(RAYMOND *appears.*)

RAYMOND: I think—he's dead.

BEN: You *think*.

SALLY: What will *you* think.

(BEN *lurches into the other room. He examines the body fairly curiously while the others wait. He reappears.*)

BEN: Cottage Hospital. Come on!

SALLY: I don't know why people make such a fuss about death. They do it all *for* you.

BEN: For you, maybe. Because you don't *know* anything.

SALLY: Yes?

BEN: Yes. You'd better be an ignorant Negro in Harlem spending a fortune.

SALLY: Oh, spare me. Promise me, if, no, when I die this year probably, a good year for me, lay me in the cold, cold ground of the smartist, sharpist, nearest, fastest furnace burning they've got.

BEN (*to* RAYMOND): Did you tell him about Sally and me?

RAYMOND: What?

BEN: What! That the whole thing was a shoddy hoax from the start. Even if it looked true to all of us, to Sally and me, it was disgusting and a hoax and an insult and a wound to everyone.

SALLY: Piety again. *You* agreed to it.

BEN: Then I was wrong. Bloody, damn wrong.

54

RAYMOND: He'd guessed already.

BEN: But you didn't disabuse him?

RAYMOND: What?

BEN: You didn't let him die better in not knowing the truth?

SALLY: Why shouldn't he know the truth. Just because he was dying? Best time to find out. Smoke out the prig, Raymond. It won't be difficult.

BEN: I'll get Jo.

SALLY: Why don't you? The field's open.

RAYMOND: Anything for anyone?

SALLY: Yes. Let's have something good—fine but robust for Glen's departure. Is there any chocolate cake?

RAYMOND: As always.

SALLY: Right. Chocolate cake and champagne. See the old thing off well before the doctor gets here. O.K. Shirley?

SHIRLEY: I love chocolate cake. Especially for breakfast. *And* champagne.

RAYMOND: Right.

(BEN *returns*.)

BEN: She won't come in. At least, till the doctor and the ambulance come.

SALLY: Probably right . . . I thought old Glen did rather well. He spent all his young years pretending to be older and all his older ones pretending to be younger. Now, *that's* a difficult feat.

BEN: I don't think you really——

SALLY: What? Yes.

BEN: Have feelings for anyone. Except dogs.

SALLY: *Your* dog.

BEN: My dog . . . How *little* you know.

SALLY: How little *you* know.

SHIRLEY: Oh, don't.

(*There is the faint huff and hoot of a small goods train on the line outside.*)

SALLY: Ah, the weekly goods that upsets Ben so much.

SHIRLEY: Early.

RAYMOND: No. Dead on time. What *can* they be shifting!

SALLY: Coffins!

55

RAYMOND: Jo's the only one——

(*They listen as the train moves through the station. Then it screeches to a stop.* BEN *runs out. They all wait.* BEN *returns with the body of* JO *in his arms.*)

BEN: She knew the time all right. I'll put her with Glen.

(*He carries her into the other room, followed by* RAYMOND.)

SALLY: I think we'll have coffee and, some will still want old English Breakfast. Hay?

(DOCTOR ASHTON *arrives at the open door.*)

ASHTON: She seems to have thrown herself right in front of the goods train. It was going slowly, but even so . . .

SALLY: Even so . . .

ASHTON: I've got the ambulance for Mr. ——

SALLY: Dear Glen. How difficult life will start to become when he and his kind, with their villas in Florence, their grasp of all things Greek disappears. Oh, and their New York apartments and erudition and all that, all that disappears, don't you think, Dr. Ashton?

ASHTON: I didn't really know much about him. He wasn't really a patient of mine.

SALLY: But you *must* have known of him. Everyone knew Glen from Berenson down to Maugham Via Cunard Junction.

ASHTON: Really?

SALLY: Really, Doctor Ashton. You must tear yourself away from the *Lancet* sometime. You'll get a very wealthy type of customer.

(*There's the sound of shooting from the railway. Glass starts to break and it is soon clear that the place is being shot up. Windows smash and things break up.*)

ASHTON: I'd better ring the police. Yobbos, I'm afraid. You, you're not popular.

SALLY: How awful to be popular.

ASHTON: Then I'd better see the patient.

SALLY: Too late, alas. Dadie Rylands, this is your life! Again.

(BEN *comes out of* GLEN's *room in an incoherent rage, shouting and rushes out on to the platform.*)

ASHTON (*on phone*): Sergeant. Oh, sorry, trouble at the old Railway halt. That's the one. Don't know, sort of yobbos,

I think. Anyway, they're smashing up the place. And I have two patients for the cottage hospital and—yes. Soon as you can . . .

(BEN *reappears, all shot up.*)

BEN: They—shot—at—the—body.

ASHTON: Yes. Two. Maybe three. Or more.

(*He examines the body of the dead* JO *while the station is shot to pieces around them.*)

Get everyone together. In the safest place . . . You've brought this on yourselves, you know.

SALLY: I dare say. If it's any comfort to you.

ASHTON: Number Three by all accounts.

BEN: RAYMOND! RAYMOND! Come and look after your Sally.

(RAYMOND *appears.*)

ASHTON: Here, give me a hand.

(RAYMOND *approaches.*)

BEN: Look after her, Raymond. I know I can rely on you . . . even when I'm *bleeding* to death.

SALLY: Oh, Ben, don't go. Don't leave me. We all, *the few of us,* need one another.

(BEN *is clearly almost dead or in a coma.*)

ASHTON: Well, you do lead odd sorts of lives, don't you.

(*The station is fast becoming a wreck and the police sirens are sounding.*)

SALLY: Yes. We do, Doctor Ashton. We do. Most of us. You must be glad.

CURTAIN